JOHN CHARLES DALY, former ABC News chief and forum moderator: This Public Policy Forum, part of a series presented by the American Enterprise Institute, is concerned with the direction of U.S. energy policy. We Americans have finally come to recognize that we have an energy problem, but we have not yet forged policies to confront and, possibly, resolve that problem.

President Carter submitted his energy message to Congress on April 20, 1977, and the Senate Republican energy initiative in opposition followed shortly thereafter. Two congressional agencies, the Congressional Research Service and the Office of Technology Assessment, challenged the completeness and accuracy of many assumptions in the Carter plan. Even before Congress weakened the Carter plan, these agencies cast doubt on whether it could have achieved its goals.

Detailed analyses of oil and gas reserves, or outlook from the Central Intelligence Agency, the Organization for Economic Cooperation and Development, and the Library of Congress each produced a different estimate and tended to make a confused picture even more so. Compounding the confusion is the fact that the controversy turns not upon energy resources alone, but also on the thorny issues of the environment, national defense, inflation, and unemployment, and of maintaining a strong and stable economy.

And so, the question is, U.S. Energy Policy: Which

Direction? Congressman Udall, as chairman of the House Committee on Interior and Insular Affairs and a member of the congressional board that governs the Office of Technology Assessment, an analytical arm of the Congress, you were very close to the energy dilemma. Do you agree with the OTA that the Carter plan has not met the challenge?

Morris K. Udall, United States Representative, Arizona: Yes and no, and let me explain. I happen to think we are in the early stages of a wrenching transition, which will be as fundamental as our turning from an agrarian society into an industrialized country.

If one looks at the energy situation from the standpoint of what has to be done over the next fifteen or twenty years as the supplies of oil and gas run out, the President's proposals were pretty timid. If one looks at them from the standpoint of what the American people are prepared to do, they are probably as bold as is possible at this time. Already, the Congress is watering down the plan. I think the general structure of the President's plan was adequate as a beginning.

Mr. Daly: Mr. Laird, you have been chairman of the National Energy Project of the American Enterprise Institute. Do you see a resolution of the energy problem in the administration's plan?

Melvin R. Laird, senior counsellor for the Reader's Digest Association and former secretary of defense: No, I don't, though I agree completely with all the conservation measures President Carter has proposed. I think the American people are ready to move forward on conservation in every aspect. I would go much further in conservation than President Carter has proposed. At the maximum, all the conservation measures will save only perhaps 9 or 10 percent of the energy we use. That is not even enough to provide jobs if Americans are to maintain their present standard of living.

U.S. ENERGY POLICY: WHICH DIRECTION?

John Charles Daly, *Moderator*

Melvin R. Laird
Edward J. Mitchell
John F. O'Leary
Morris K. Udall

A Round Table held on June 27, 1977
and sponsored by
the American Enterprise Institute for Public Policy Research
Washington, D.C.

AEI Forum 8

ISBN 0-8447-2102-6
Library of Congress Catalog Card No. 77-83115
Printed in the United States of America

The emphasis should be on production. I would not quarrel with any conservation measures, and I would go beyond the conservation program of President Carter. I advocated rationing two and a half years ago.

Conservation is good—it is needed, and it is necessary—but it is not the answer to America's energy needs for the next ten years. We have to move toward more production. We have no energy shortage in America. We have a production shortage, and it can be solved.

Mr. Daly: Mr. O'Leary, as chief of the Federal Energy Administration, you may well be described as a close relative of the baby, the Carter plan. Have the congressional debate and the general dialogue of the past months raised any doubts as to the merits of the program?

John F. O'Leary, administrator of the Federal Energy Administration: No. I think that the plan is basically sound. It does the things that Mr. Laird says we ought to be doing—that is, to conserve and to find new supplies—more effectively than anything else proposed in recent years. It has very, very strong incentives for additional coal production, as well as for increased production of oil and gas. It seems to be the right balance of strong measures—measures aimed at conservation and at eliciting new supplies.

Mr. Daly: Professor Mitchell, you wrote *U.S. Energy Policy: A Primer* for the American Enterprise Institute, and you served as the executive director of President Nixon's energy committee five years ago. Is the United States making progress in resolving its energy problems, in your view?

Edward J. Mitchell, professor of business economics, University of Michigan: No, I do not think we are making any progress at all. In fact, I am rather depressed about the situation. I think we have gone backwards.

I did not particularly find the Nixon program terribly

appealing, but the Carter program heads off, in most cases, in the opposite direction. The stress on conservation is overdone. *Conservation* is an abstract noun for doing without, and is a response to scarcity that does not particularly commend itself.

A large part of the problem has to do with past government policies that have been continued, policies that tend to induce shortages of supplies in this country. Those policies must be changed if we are to get out of trouble in the energy market.

Mr. Daly: Mr. Laird, you had very strong and pronounced views of the weaknesses in the Carter plan. If you were in charge of putting together a complete program to resolve the energy problem, how would you handle it?

Mr. Laird: First, I would stress the need for conservation. I have no quarrel with that. But I would return to a market economy as far as energy is concerned.

We have an abundance of coal and uranium. We have a shortage of gas and oil. If we are going to solve this problem, we should encourage production, and the way to encourage production is to return to a free market economy.

When I visited Great Britain recently, some of my old friends there were very encouraged by the tremendous production of oil that is coming on the line. They are talking about a price per barrel of about $21.00 by 1981 and $27.50 by 1985.

The Carter energy proposal pegs all of our energy requirements to the prices set by the Organization of Petroleum Exporting Countries, and it sets a tax against the American production based upon the OPEC price. The American consumer pays these tremendous taxes, which now amount to some $14 billion per year. The American energy price derives from a tax differential based upon OPEC prices, and the OPEC countries are joined by Great Britain, Norway, Venezuela, and some other countries.

That policy just accepts OPEC control of our energy program.

We can make the change to coal and uranium, and we can move forward towards solar power and other more sophisticated types of energy in the year 2000 and beyond. But we have to solve the energy problem of the next fifteen years, and we should not base our whole system on OPEC prices, as the Carter program does.

Mr. Daly: Let me ask a question here as a layman. Is OPEC a cartel? Isn't a cartel a grouping together to control a market in order to create an artificial price for a product?

Mr. O'Leary: I smiled when Mr. Laird called for the return to a free market. I have been in this business long enough to know that we have not had a free market for petroleum in the United States since about 1933 or 1934, when the federal government, under the National Recovery Administration and some later legislation, moved to counteract a very depressed price situation. From that time until 1972, the U.S. government maintained prices higher than world market prices. There were no complaints about market interference in 1960 or 1965, when a $3.00 price was held in a $1.00 world, but there are bitter complaints now about holding an $11.00 price in a $13.50 world.

Mr. Laird: We did complain, though, back in 1969 and 1970. I took a minority viewpoint that the price of $2.25 for oil could not be depended upon and that we should be encouraging production in the United States.

Mr. O'Leary: By holding the price at three times the world market price, we were trying to do precisely that. The fact of the matter is the domestic oil industry simply let our reserves run down during that period. In 1965, we had 3 million barrels a day of excess capacity in this country—the hangover, if you will, of an enormous surge in drilling that had taken place years before. By 1970, the last barrel of that excess capacity had been used up. Through the policy of keeping that price up, we had effectively drained the United States first.

CONGRESSMAN UDALL: There is a great irony about the free market people—the people who preach about the free market but don't practice it. Until April 1973, there were countries standing in line trying to sell us $1.00 oil or $1.50 oil, and do you know what the policy of the Johnson, Kennedy, and Nixon administrations was? Our national policy was to keep out all that cheap oil in order to maintain high oil prices in this country. The strategy, apparently, was to pump out and burn up our oil as fast as we could, and not to rely on free market forces to keep prices down.

I get a little unhappy about free market talk, especially when it comes from our oil companies, who are really part of the cartel. They deal with the OPEC countries on behalf of the United States. In bargaining for Saudi oil, Exxon has to face the question of whether the price of oil should go from $14.00 a barrel to $16.00 a barrel. Exxon has 3 billion barrels of oil reserves in the ground. If that price goes up $2.00 a barrel, they have made $6 billion that day without getting out of bed. What incentive is there to bargain for lower prices? I am for the free market, but let's really practice it and not just preach it. And let's break up the oil companies—that's the way to get some competition into our system.

PROFESSOR MITCHELL: As one who both preaches and practices free markets, and always has, I find this the strangest kind of argument—that in the past we kept the price of oil above the free market level, and that was wrong, so we will rectify that today by keeping the price of oil in the United States below the world market level. In other words, we are saying we made a terrible mistake in the past—we propped up the price in the United States and had enormous surpluses as a result. Every advocate of a free market believes that policy was wrong. But how can anyone say that now we must correct that error by pricing domestic oil below the world market level? That does not help in any way.

CONGRESSMAN UDALL: The strength of the Carter program on this tax is based on a simple proposition. Over the next two years, the American people will pay $20 billion or $30 billion in increased prices for oil, and they have three choices: they can either pay that $20 billion to OPEC, or they can pay some of it to the seven big oil companies in the United States, or they can pay it to themselves through a tax, because the U.S. price will go up to the world price, one way or another. If the regulations come off, the U.S. price will float immediately up to $14 a barrel. The American people cannot afford to send that money abroad to OPEC or to the oil companies. Neither of them needs it as much as the American people need it.

MR. LAIRD: But don't you think the American people need energy?

CONGRESSMAN UDALL: Yes.

MR. LAIRD: Don't you think we need jobs?

CONGRESSMAN UDALL: Yes, we do.

MR. LAIRD: Don't you think the United States should maintain its standard of living at its current level? How can we move to coal, uranium, and other sources of energy if we maintain cheap prices for scarce products. That does not provide answers or solutions.

For instance, in the near future some exemptions will be granted to power plants in California giving them contracts for natural gas at a very low price. Three years ago, the Nixon administration wanted thirty-eight power plants to change to coal, but not a single one has changed—not a single one in three years—because they have a cheap energy source. The only way they will change is not through the courts or through legislation but rather through the free market place.

Mr. O'Leary: Mr. Laird, let's just examine that just a moment. These are gas-fired plants. They are not coal-fired or oil-fired plants; in fact, they cannot burn coal. It is not a matter of asking for the plants to be changed. What has to be done is to close down each gas-fired plant and build one right next door to it that will run on coal.

The situation is rigged in this country, because there is a purchase fuel adjustment clause in virtually every public service commission's regulatory armory. That clause says a utility can pay anything within reason—and we have not come to the edges of reason yet—for gas or for oil, and it can channel that extra cost through to the customer.

Gas currently costs relatively little in California. But in Texas, gas is very close to the clearing price for oil. Coal can be brought into Texas for about half the price of oil or gas. The utility companies in Texas will not shift to coal because they can get the additional money for oil or gas very easily from their customers. But it is very, very difficult for the utilities to get a rate increase that permits them to invest the capital to build the new coal-fired plant to replace that gas-fired plant.

The situation is very, very complicated, and there is no way simple market forces can compel a regulated industry such as the utilities to switch, because they have built-in cushions that allow them not to switch on the basis of fuel price.

Professor Mitchell: Congressman Udall made a point about the money going to oil companies. I do not see how we will develop more energy sources in this country unless money goes to the oil companies. They are the ones that produce the oil and gas that is the primary source of energy in the United States. How can we get more energy without paying for it?

Congressman Udall: Well, I'm for oil companies. We need oil companies, and in this day and age, they have to be pretty big. I want them to make some money. More oil and gas can be found, but not as much as some think. That is not the answer, because supplies are declining. Finding the remainder is a job, though, and I want oil companies to make a bundle of money doing it.

What I object to is companies with oil and gas in the ground that was produced under old costs. Suddenly, because of changes in the law and some false belief in market forces, what is $3.00 oil today becomes $6.00 oil tomorrow.

Mr. Daly: What about the man who bought a house for $20,000 ten years ago and can sell it now for $100,000? Is that not the same equation? I'm just asking for information.

Congressman Udall: Sure, but we do not give homeowners the kind of monopoly control and power that we give oil companies, and that is the difference. They run our lives in many fundamental ways, and they shouldn't.

I am for shifting to market forces gradually, but not under the existing natural gas markets. If someone who owns a gas well in Texas wants to shop around to see who wants to buy the gas, he may find only one buyer—a big system of interstate gathering lines in that area. He either sells at their price or he does not sell at all. Market forces do not apply to the giant conglomerate oil companies, as though they were seven drugstores in which any customer can shop. That notion is sadly mistaken.

Mr. Laird: It is nice to blame the oil and the gas industry for all these problems. That is an easy way out.

The problem, though, is to solve what people refer to as

an energy crisis. I think it is a public policy crisis in that people are unwilling to do what is necessary—to make the shifts and create the means by which we supply our energy. By putting on the embargo, the Arabs did us a great favor in many ways. It should have alerted us.

CONGRESSMAN UDALL: I hope they don't do us these favors very often. [Laughter.]

MR. LAIRD: It should have alerted us to the fact that we are very dependent upon foreign sources of energy. And, from a national security standpoint, from an economic standpoint, and from any other standpoint, that was bad for the United States.

Yet, what has happened since the embargo? The amount of Arab oil imported into the United States has gone up 5 to 6 percent every year. We are importing up to 41 percent of our oil right now. We are not making the shifts to other sources of power.

In Wisconsin, my home state, 30 percent of our power comes from nuclear energy. The next major source of power is coal. Drivers on the interstate highway between Madison and Minneapolis can see two fine, big coal plants. But they cannot see anything coming out of those stacks, with their great, new scrubbers. We have taken steps in Wisconsin to become independent of oil and gas.

Many areas of this country are refusing to make these changes, and that concerns me. What is the best incentive that can be provided to make the change from oil and gas to other energy sources? I think it is the marketplace, but perhaps not. If there is another solution, we should hear it.

CONGRESSMAN UDALL: Of course, we need incentives. Market forces are tidy and neat, and they do the job better than any other kind of system, but market forces are not always appropriate. The 1973 Arab oil embargo was a wrenching experience for the United States. It led to unemployment,

10

the whole round of energy inflation, and higher energy prices. And what you want to do is turn the ratchet and spring a free market in gas and oil on us, when it has been a controlled market all these years. The price we would pay would be another recession, another round of energy inflation, and a slowdown in getting the clean alternative sources of energy that you want and I want.

Mr. Laird: That is not what I want. I want to make a change in the basic source of energy in America. I do not want to have to rely on natural gas and oil, but we are continuing to rely on them, and that is a mistake.

Mr. O'Leary: Mr. Laird, the keystone of the President's program is a series of initiatives to make industry and the utilities shift from oil and gas to coal.

The administration's objective is to increase the burn of coal between now and 1985 by about 550 million tons, which is equivalent to today's production and use of steam coal in this country.

Mr. Laird: I don't think that will happen. I wish it would happen, but I don't think it will.

Mr. O'Leary: Those who have analyzed the program, Mr. Laird, including the Congressional Budget Office and the Library of Congress, say that it will, within very narrow limits, happen. President Carter's national energy plan provides precisely the incentives you are calling for. Why will industry shift? Because it will be taxed until it will gain from a shift. That is precisely what you are calling for.

Let me ask you this: Why should we shift $35 billion from the consumers to the producers of this country? That is implicit in your plan—$35 billion to the oil and gas producers, with as much as $4 billion going to one company. The entire expenditure for exploration by the oil industry today is on the order of $10 billion, and for drilling, it is about $2.5 billion. And, Mr. Laird, right now, every drill that can be used in this country is being fully utilized.

MR. LAIRD: We would have to have a windfall profits tax on oil and gas companies if we returned to a free market. We would have to establish some sort of means like the food stamp program. Perhaps we need an energy stamp program. That can be worked out under a free market system. The problem is that this change is not being encouraged. No mechanism has been set up to handle environmental impact studies effectively, efficiently, and fast. All of the environmental decisions, along with the energy decisions, are being passed from the agencies to the President. The President of the United States cannot be expected to make those trade-offs, but, under this program, all of them must be made by him. There is no real trade-off before decisions reach him. That sort of organization will not be effective and efficient in making the hard, tough decisions that are needed.

MR. O'LEARY: Mr. Laird, you must be referring to some plan other than the one I am working from. These decisions have been made to date by a partnership between the Environmental Protection Agency and the Federal Energy Administration. As a matter of fact, between now and the end of the week we will issue another thirty or forty orders. They do not go to the President.

MR. LAIRD: I am glad that you are making those decisions. I have not seen these thirty or forty decisions that will be made in the next week, but I congratulate you on finally making some decisions.

MR. O'LEARY: We have only been in office for about five months.

MR. LAIRD: I congratulate you for moving forward on thirty and forty decisions for next week, because there have been no decisions in the last five months.

12

Professor Mitchell: I think we are ignoring how we got into this problem. We are talking here as if OPEC arose out of nothing.

The federal government, beginning in the early 1960s with natural gas and then in the early 1970s with oil, deliberately curtailed supply in this country. It is hardly surprising that a country curtailing the supply of its basic energy source winds up importing great quantities from abroad. And, if that production abroad is concentrated in one or two countries, a cartel might arise. It is incorrect to speak about this cartel as if it is a fact of life that simply arose. It is in part a creation of U.S. energy policy. That policy is being continued under the Carter plan. Market prices are still not being charged for oil and gas in this country. Congressman Udall said the market is not competitive or free, but there is competition in the pipeline market. Twenty-five years ago, there were a few places with only a single pipeline, but nowadays that is generally not the case. And, if there is only a single pipeline going into an area and many producers, the price of gas will be below the competitive level, not above it.

In this country, we have not had a period with a free market for natural gas. In recent times, we have had it only in the intrastate market, and that market has behaved remarkably well. In that market, prices rose when they were supposed to rise and fell when they were supposed to fall. Industry in those parts of the country has done extremely well. And, under the Carter plan, the one free market that has been allowed to survive will be eliminated.

That says something about the plan. When I look at the plan, I do not see an economic rationale to it. All I see is that every little free market that might flourish will be controlled. That seems to be the theme of the policy.

Mr. O'Leary: Let me describe that market to you. The price went up between 1970 and 1977 by a factor of ten—from $.17 per million cubic feet to $1.75 roughly. The rate of activity, the employment of rigs, more than doubled, from 300 in 1970 to about 650 today. The reason no more are being used today is because there are no more.

And what happened to the footage drilled? It went up by 60 percent. The number of wells completed went from about 8,000 to about 13,000 a year. And then what happened to production? In each of the years since then, with one exception for oil, production of both oil and gas has gone down.

This tells us something about the sort of resource we are working with in this country. It is a resource that has been pretty well worked over. What has to be done, and what the President's program does, is to find ways to get this very, very strong industry, the oil industry, to explore new areas and drill deep down. That is what I meant when I said that the incentives under our proposal are stronger than they would be under deregulation.

PROFESSOR MITCHELL: The facts you have presented are very misleading. First of all, the price of natural gas was incredibly low because nobody looked for natural gas in bygone days..To say it went up tenfold is to say nothing because it began almost at zero.

Furthermore, to say that production has not increased enormously in that market is just to recognize that it is a small market. On the producing side there may be enormous potential, but the intrastate market represents demand in only a handful of states. What would happen in that market in terms of prices, consumption, and production if the entire U.S. market were uncontrolled would be quite another thing.

CONGRESSMAN UDALL: My conservative friends embrace a fallacy, and I don't know when they will turn loose of it. The centerpiece of the whole Nixon-Ford energy program was more production. If those oil companies were just turned loose, they would get consumers all the oil and gas they needed—that was at the heart of the policy, although there was some emphasis on other things as well.

The Carter policy turns its back on that and accepts the proposition that we live in a finite world. Natural gas peaked in 1972 or 1973. Whether the price is $2.00 or $200 per thousand cubic feet for natural gas, there will never be more gas produced than in 1973.

PROFESSOR MITCHELL: What is the basis of that statement?

CONGRESSMAN UDALL: They tell us we are crying wolf. In 1920 some experts said we were running out of oil, and we didn't run out of oil. In the 1930s, people said we would run out of oil, and we didn't. Now, in the 1970s, the cry is we are running out of oil, and we are told it still will not happen. But it took millions of years to put this oil on earth and no price and no amount of drilling can produce any more oil than there is on this planet. It is a finite amount, and we are nearing the limits of it. In our lifetime we will see the exhaustion of most of the remaining supplies of oil and gas at $10.00 a barrel or $110 or $1,010 a barrel. We are running out, and we must face that fact. We must get rid of the idea that somehow our problems will go away if we give oil companies more big profits and turn them loose. They will not.

PROFESSOR MITCHELL: To say that it is finite is to say nothing.

MR. LAIRD: Profits can be controlled by a windfall profits tax. My interest is in making the conversion, not being dependent upon gas and oil, and I do not think Congressman Udall addressed that problem. Price will encourage people to make the conversion. It will encourage our states, our communities, and our country to make the conversion.

MR. DALY: We have had some discussion of coal but very little on the issue of atomic fuel. Why are we not going where we expected to go twenty years ago? We had thought by this time in our history nuclear power plants would be playing a substantial role.

Congressman Udall: I believe in this. We ought to apply it wherever we can, but we ought not to apply it where it does not fit. We ought to have nuclear power competing with coal, and we ought to have coal competing with oil, and we ought to have solar energy competing with all of them across the board. But simply to raise the prices of oil and gas out of sight and let OPEC fix our prices instead of some kind of vague, dreamy, free market forces, to me is a serious conceptual mistake.

Mr. Daly: Let me ask a dumb layman's question. Mr. Laird said OPEC fixed our prices, and I need an explanation. Mr. O'Leary probably can give it to me. Canada is selling us gas now at $2.00 a thousand cubic feet.

Mr. O'Leary: $2.16.

Mr. Daly: $2.16. It is going up steadily.

Mr. O'Leary: Yes, $1.90 yesterday; $2.16 today. It simply follows the B.t.u. equivalent from OPEC.

Mr. Daly: So that the Canadians are dictating that in the same context that OPEC is?

Mr. O'Leary: No, they are responding to—

Mr. Laird: No, they are staying with OPEC—Great Britain is staying with OPEC. Norway will stay with OPEC. They will all stay with OPEC. If the United States is to make the conversions that are necessary, the way to do it is through price.

Mr. O'Leary: I agree with you, and the President's program does precisely that. The price to a utility as a consumer of oil or gas in this country will be the OPEC price, plus.

16

Professor Mitchell: But not to a producer.

Mr. Laird: Not to a consumer.

Mr. O'Leary: No, let's stick with the issue now. If a man developed an oil field thirty or forty years ago and paid for it three years later, why should we pay him $13.50 a barrel? What economic function is performed by that? The new oil field in this country will bring the OPEC price. Now, what could be better than that?

Professor Mitchell: It is a fallacy to assume that someone who developed a field thirty or forty years ago expected the same price for thirty or forty years. The price of old oil has not even maintained itself in real terms. Anyone that developed a field some years ago would at least have expected the same real price, and he is not getting it. Most producers of old oil are suffering windfall losses.

Mr. O'Leary: Most producers of old oil who suffer windfall losses have an escape hatch. They can come to the FEA and go through an appeals procedure. Indeed, we got 400 appeals last year and said okay to a half of them. The procedure is being used.

Professor Mitchell: How can you possibly make such a judgment?

Mr. O'Leary: They open their books to us. You brought up windfall losses. The best estimate we can make is that the profit, the clear profit on that old oil, averages nationally about $2.00, and for the $13.50 price, the return to the producer on a new oil field in this country under the President's program is higher than the return to the producer in any other part of the world.

Mr. Laird: How high does the price have to get before we decide to make the shifts? How high does OPEC have to go?

MR. O'LEARY: Mr. Laird, I keep saying that the administration's program will take the OPEC price plus to the industrialists and the utilities and, at that point, market forces will tell us how that works.

MR. LAIRD: West Germany got no real conservation or cutback until the price of a gallon of gas rose to $1.50.

MR. O'LEARY: Now, you are thinking about gasoline?

MR. LAIRD: Yes.

MR. O'LEARY: Historically the price of gasoline in Germany has been very high, and the response of the people has been to buy small, efficient cars relative to ours.

Over time, adding a nickel and another nickel and another nickel will take some people out of the market. A massive change does not happen all of a sudden. The price goes up a little and nothing happens; it goes up some more and nothing happens; and still it goes up and nothing happens. Then, all of a sudden, something happens. Something actually is happening at each point along that curve.

MR. LAIRD: But it just started happening after $1.50. When the price of gasoline got up to about $1.82, there was some reduction in demand.

MR. O'LEARY: That is right. It is interesting to note in that context that today's price of gasoline in the U.S. market in real terms is equivalent to the 1960 price.

MR. LAIRD: And that is not encouraging conservation.

MR. O'LEARY: I agree. We made a proposal to the Congress to handle this, and the Congress turned it down.

CONGRESSMAN UDALL: I am one of those lonely congressmen who thought the standby gas tax was a pretty good idea. I am prepared to vote for it today because that nickel or dime or fifteen cents sends a message.

When the gas pump registers $18.00 and not $16.00 not much of an impression is made. But if it is $20.00, or $22.00, not $16.00, that sends a message. It says to buy a house closer to one's work. It says double up. It says join a carpool. It says look at mass transit. It sends messages every time gasoline is bought.

The change will not be dramatic—we will not wake up some morning and find a dramatic shift, as Mr. O'Leary says. But the cumulative effect over time of all of those messages to 200 million Americans will bear real fruit from the standpoint of conservation.

MR. DALY: We have not yet touched on the question of nuclear fuel. Why has its performance in twenty years been so disappointing. Does the administration program remove the roadblocks that have held nuclear energy down?

CONGRESSMAN UDALL: My friend Mel Laird wants to talk about competition in market forces, so maybe he can tell us why those friendly folks at Gulf Oil, who have done so much to purify our political process in recent years, joined a cartel to drive uranium prices from $7.00 or $8.00 up to $40.00 per ton. Where is the competition there? This is what worries me.

MR. LAIRD: You don't expect me to support that, do you?

CONGRESSMAN UDALL: No, no. [Laughter.] But the plain fact is that the great dream of cheap, abundant nuclear power, which dominated thinking about energy in the 1950s and 1960s, is not really credible anymore. Nuclear power will play a role in our lives. We have 10 or 11 percent of our electrical energy generated by it now, and it may go to 15 or 16 or 18 percent. But that great dream of abundant and cheap nuclear power has encountered problems. So has coal. So has everything we turn to. But nuclear energy is not the answer for economic reasons and because of increasing citizen concern about safety, and a whole range of other things.

Mr. Daly: In your recommendations, Mr. Laird, in the publication by the American Enterprise Institute, you take particular interest in the fact that environmental concerns could hold up progress in increasing production over substantial periods of time.

Mr. Laird: The procedures for reviewing nuclear power plants and writing environmental impact statements have to be modernized. The procedures for protecting the environment are necessary, but they should not be set up so that decisions cannot be made.

Tonight we learned that there will be forty or fifty decisions in the next week in this area. That is the best news we have had on this program, because no decisions have been made before. We have been at a standstill, and now we will move forward. I think that is great news.

Congressman Udall: The House Committee on Interior and Insular Affairs held hearings, and Mr. O'Leary was one of the witnesses on why it takes ten years to get a nuclear plant on line producing energy from the day the decision is made to build it.

There are also problems in building a coal plant. We have been building coal plants for years, but we build them only a year and a half or two years faster now. Maybe Mel Laird and I can agree on something here. If society has decided, through its regular processes of consultation, that we must have more nuclear plants, then there ought to be a piece of paper that says yes, that plant can be built.

The General Accounting Office studied this question and concluded that the ten-year cycle consists of six years of construction time, two years of preparation for construction (picking the site and arranging the financing), and two years of regulatory delay.

20

So, if there were someone with a stamp who could approve an application immediately, and the construction workers began work at once, there would still be an eight-year delay. It is a very long time. These are very big and very complicated plants. We owe the country a better and more simplified decision-making process, but that will not totally eliminate the long lead time necessary to build big nuclear or coal plants.

MR. LAIRD: But the time can be cut back.

CONGRESSMAN UDALL: The reductions can be made, and we ought to look for them.

MR. DALY: In the area of solar energy, I wonder if the public understanding of its potential is not out of whack. By accident or otherwise, the public has come to expect too much from it. It is essentially supplemental, isn't it?

MR. O'LEARY: There are really two sides to this. First of all, the experts were telling us four years ago that, let's say, $1,000 spent for an installed kilowatt per hour of capacity of nuclear power would be equivalent to $100,000 for the same capacity of solar electric power. Within five years, we are finding that $100,000 ought to be down to $3,000 or $4,000, and that is an enormously important statement. That means that if we must go to solar energy, we can do it with about the same jolt to the economy that we suffered during 1973 and 1974 in terms of basic energy costs.

But there will be no massive deployment of solar energy tomorrow morning for household heating, though there may be a massive deployment for domestic hot water heating. We are about ready for that. I would put the household heating at some five to ten years down the road, as energy costs generally go up and improved technology reduces them.

The really important developments have occurred in

the area of photoelectric production of electrical energy. That has gone down at a rate that none of us in the business could have predicted three years ago.

MR. DALY: I think we have covered much of the subject. If no one wants to go into other areas I think it is about time that we go to the question and answer session.

ARTHUR J. MORRIS, chief executive officer of Capital Energy Resources Corporation: Mr. O'Leary, are we paying enough attention to certain esoteric forms of energy sources, like the development of hydrogen, for when we run out of oil and coal and also for the protection of our environment in the future?

MR. O'LEARY: Probably not, but you have to understand that hydrogen is probably not going to be a source of energy. It is going to be a means, a medium of energy. That is, there is an awful lot of hydrogen in sea water, but to get to it, a lot of energy has to be used in the form of chemical or electrical processes, and then no more energy can be obtained than is put in it, even at 100 percent efficiency. I tend to be less than optimistic about the spread of the hydrogen economy.

DONALD BRADLEY, Federal Energy Administration: We have heard a lot about increasing energy production here in this country, but we have set up a massive strategic oil reserve program. We buy oil and pump it into large caverns here in this country as a reserve. Some of this oil will undoubtedly come from foreign sources. I wonder about the logic of buying oil at high prices from foreign sources and pumping it into the ground here. At the same time, we raise production here by paying many small producers through

FEA's exemption process the maximum price per barrel to pump oil out of the ground.

And a related question: Why, if we are so concerned with consumption, do we want to initiate a massive increase in production here? Would it not be better to leave our oil underground and buy from foreign producers?

CONGRESSMAN UDALL: The strategic oil reserve is an insurance policy. The United States paid a frightful price in 1973-1974 during the Arab oil embargo, and if we are suddenly confronted with another embargo, we want to have a six-month supply of imports on hand to get us through.

The basic rationale for a reserve now is that oil will never again be as cheap as it is today. If you think $14.00 is bad, try $24.00 or $34.00, because over the next decade or so prices can only go up.

If a reserve is needed, it may as well be established while the price is $14.00 rather than waiting until it is higher.

I question whether there is any real need to dash out and ransack the outer continental shelf as fast as we can and burn all of that oil up. I agree with you that we really need to use wisely our remaining oil and gas. If we take the view some do that all the oil and gas we need is out there—or that all we want is out there, and we only need higher prices—then it makes no difference how fast it is developed.

But if we take the view that the supply is declining, then the best policy is to act carefully and husband our resources to stretch them out as long as possible.

MR. O'LEARY: It couldn't have been said any better by the fellow who initiated this whole program. [Laughter.]

PROFESSOR MITCHELL: I do think Congressman Udall expressed one misconception. The problems created by the 1973-1974 embargo were largely the result not of the embargo, but of the Federal Energy Office. Many countries that rely much more heavily on oil from embargoed countries did not have nearly as many problems as we had.

MR. O'LEARY: Professor Mitchell should remember that right now unemployment in Great Britain is still very, very substantial because of that embargo. The economic bite on the world economy has been well documented, and his point in this regard is simply not well taken.

PROFESSOR MITCHELL: I totally disagree with you. The unemployment in Britain is not directly traceable to the Arab oil embargo.

ALAN LUDWIG, Forum for the Advancement of Students in Science and Technology (FASST): My question, for Mr. O'Leary and anybody else who would care to respond to it, involves energy education. An organization such as FASST has a chance to attend many energy conferences. Unfortunately, a great number of people do not have an opportunity to hear the experts and participate in these give-and-take sessions. What is being done in the national energy plan to deal with energy education, so that people can understand what in the hell you all are talking about at these sessions?

What will be done to make the people understand that energy is not a discipline, that it is something that encompasses our entire life? Can they be taught to understand the litany of the language that is thrown around? Do those of us involved in energy education have to wait until the Department of Energy comes into being before we can get proposals funded and approved? What will be done in the meantime?

MR. DALY: First we should note that there is no lack of energy in the nether regions to which you referred, and then if you will take it, Mr. O'Leary.

MR. O'LEARY: This is an area that has to be addressed very carefully. There is a difference between education and propaganda that has to be bridged.

In the past the FEA has conducted educational programs on, for example, deregulation of gas that had been interpreted by the Congress as essentially propaganda—not really education but, rather, furthering a point of view.

My own view on this is that we should move very cautiously. We should go into the outreach program that is now being developed. We should go to the people who are helping spread technical information to the farms. The most counterproductive thing we could do is to damage the government's credibility until people simply do not believe us.

We are spending a good bit of money on workshops around the country. We are reaching executives of conservation programs in some 600 workshops aimed at hard applications—not rhetoric but hard application. Each workshop will probably reach between twenty-five and fifty executives, so we reach a good many people that way.

There are many other FEA programs of this nature now going forward. Each, though, is cautiously executed so it does not cross the line between propaganda and education.

PROFESSOR MITCHELL: Mr. O'Leary's point is very well taken. Before Mr. O'Leary was associated with FEA, many of the things it put out to explain the energy crisis were examples of economic fallacies and how not to use economic analysis. FEA should proceed very cautiously on that kind of thing.

MR. LAIRD: Mr. O'Leary blames the unemployment problem in Great Britain on the Arab embargo. I spent quite a little time in Great Britain, and none of the economists or politicians I talked to made that point. If the Federal Energy Administration put out that sort of information, it would be jumped on very hard. You have to be careful with that kind of propaganda, Mr. O'Leary. [Laughter.]

Mr. O'Leary: Mr. Laird, I keep in touch, as you may well imagine, with British officials from time to time, and I hear quite the other story. So your statement might have been propaganda. [Laughter.]

Jacqueline Tillman, American Enterprise Institute: This evening, there has been quite a considerable amount of discussion regarding big, mass solutions to the energy problem. What weight in national energy policy is being given to the small, but beautiful and perhaps troublesome, approach to solving our energy needs—perhaps regional and decentralized approaches—you know, the windmill here, the solar heated house here, the dam there?

Congressman Udall: I am glad you raised that subject. The American people like the big, sexy, exotic solution—they like it when someone comes charging out of the laboratory and says the giant nuclear power plant, or hydrogen, or something else is the answer, and our problems are over.

I suspect we will look back fifteen or twenty years from now and realize that we did not have a solution but a whole bunch of solutions. Nuclear energy will help us a little, and conservation will be a big help. Some of these hydrogen units that Mr. O'Leary was talking about will help some, and solar energy will play a bigger and bigger role. We will see wind power, and burning garbage, and maybe even firewood, but we ought to think of smaller solutions, decentralized solutions, and not look to one giant plant somewhere cranking out nuclear fusion, or some other big solution. We should be looking for a lot of little solutions. We ought to finance the little basement inventor and the small company that come up with many applications. To take just one idea, I had a fellow in my office not too long ago who pointed out that there are 300 million electrical engines working in the United States. One little retrofit device would make an engine do the same amount of work with half the electrical current. That could play a big role.

PROFESSOR MITCHELL: One of the nice things about a market that is not regulated by the FEA or some other agency is that people are free to do such things. They are quite free to try them—companies are free to make such things, and consumers are free to use them.

What I find strange is that the administration feels the necessity to subsidize things like solar power. If solar energy has a place in the market, it will find that place. The FEA or any other body should not feel called upon to decide which of these new sources should be subsidized and which should not, and which should be taxed, and so forth.

JACK KOLE, *Milwaukee Journal:* This question has been alluded to but really not answered directly. Could I ask each one of the panelists whether the profits of the large oil companies currently are too high or too low, or do they consider them reasonable?

PROFESSOR MITCHELL: While oil company profits have fluctuated—and they have been higher in the last couple of years than in the past—on average over a long period of time, they have been close to the norm for all manufacturing corporations. Further, any number of studies show from every angle that oil company profits over the long pull have been normal profits.

MR. LAIRD: I agree with Professor Mitchell. Looked at on a long-term basis, the profits have been reasonable and on the same basis as other sections of industry over the last twenty years.

CONGRESSMAN UDALL: I think the oil company profits are high, outrageously so. I think the level of profits ought to be fixed by market forces. If people need something it should be produced in a competitive atmosphere so that someone can make some money on it. That is the amount that ought to be made. But there is no competition. The big oil companies have been protected by government, and kept out of the competitive market. They tend to cooperate with OPEC, and become involved, as Gulf did, with fixing the price of uranium.

That is why I would break up the oil companies and make them spin off a production division, a pipeline division, a refinery division, and a marketing division. Then they could compete with other refineries, and other marketing organizations, and other pipelines, and so on. Then, their profits would be valid, whereas now, they are shielded. We do not even know what the oil companies' true profits are because they do so much double-entry bookkeeping and have so many joint ventures and subsidies and interlocking relations with foreign companies.

I think their profits are too high. As I said earlier, the oil companies ought to make a bundle of money finding oil and gas, but it ought to be earned on a competitive basis so that we would know the profits were not outrageous.

MR. O'LEARY: The question has some elements of a shell game to it, and we should ask ourselves, Where is the pea? The pea is not the profits, oddly enough.

Mr. Laird and Professor Mitchell are correct in saying that the expressed profits of the oil industry have been in line, more or less, with those of other manufacturers, until their inventory gain was so great in 1974 that they simply could not put it into other forms of investment fast enough.

Generally speaking, the shell to look under is the capital expansion shell. In that area the oil industry has done marvelously, to the point where fifteen out of the top sixteen rated corporations in this country are oil companies. The question should be not about profits, but about how the companies are doing, and they are doing marvelously.

MR. LAIRD: You are not against them?

MR. O'LEARY: No, it's just an observation.

Mr. Laird: I thought you gave the impression that you might be—

Mr. O'Leary: Not a bit. Let's just ask the right question.

Mr. Laird: But you would like to have them do well?

Mr. O'Leary: I would like to have all U.S. industry competitively pitted against one another and doing well.

Mr. Laird: That is the way I feel.

Mr. O'Leary: I think competition may not always have been present in the oil industry.

Professor Mitchell: I cannot let this go on. Where is this study, this analysis, that shows that the oil company profits have been extremely high? Any number of studies have been done, but I have never heard companies rated according to how well they do simply by capital expansion. What is the relevance of that to the competitiveness of the industry?

Mr. O'Leary: Professor Mitchell, sometime you ought to get one of the people in your class to make a comparative analysis, for a graduate exercise, of the capital growth of the oil industry in comparison with other U. S. industries. What will be found is that the tax laws granting a depletion allowance and an intangible drilling expense permitted the oil companies to convert what would have been a profit in a normal industry practice, into an investment, more or less tax-free. This opportunity has been exploited handsomely by the oil industry. That has been one of the secrets of the enormous capital growth of the U.S. oil industry.

Professor Mitchell: There is no secret here. We do not have to measure profits by accounting statements. And by the way, double-entry bookkeeping is what all firms use and have always used.

Congressman Udall: Triple, they use triple and quadruple. [Laughter.]

Professor Mitchell: Accounting data need not be relied on; we have market data. People can invest; people have bought oil companies. People own them. They get dividends and they get stock price appreciation. Profits can be analyzed that way. There is nothing hidden there. A company either has to pay the money out or keep it in the firm.

Any responsible financial analysis of that industry supports the conclusion that Mr. Laird and I have just expressed. And I find it extraordinary to keep hearing statements to the contrary made without explicit reference to some serious study.

Mr. O'Leary: Would you care to make explicit reference to the serious study that says the profitability has not been substantial?

Professor Mitchell: I have done studies myself and published them. I would be happy to send them to you. And there are others—Professor Erikson of North Carolina State University, and Professor Shyam Sunder, of the University of Chicago, have done studies. Studies have been done over and over. The Federal Trade Commission publishes data. Organizations and advocates on the other side have done studies, but I have never seen one with anything to contradict this conclusion.

Mr. O'Leary: Let me give you just one measure of the difficulty I have in being that fanatic about this situation. I was testifying before a congressional committee just the other day with Mr. Dunham, the chairman of the Federal Power Commission, who was asked the basis upon which the commission set a price of $1.44 for new gas under its order of July 1976. His answer was that on the basis of twenty-five years of FPC studies of the profitability, the cost, and so on, of the oil industry, the commission received staff advice that would have justified pricing new gas anywhere between 60 cents and $2.40.

In view of that, I think we lack an understanding of the finances in the oil industry. We do have the phenomenon of enormous growth. I have been charged by the Congress to get the financial data to put this question to rest for good and all. Meanwhile, any assertion that oil companies are not profitable is arguable, as are any assertions that they are extremely profitable.

PROFESSOR MITCHELL: I assume you are aware of the field called finance, which is taught at universities. Scholars in that field have looked at all these matters. I will be interested to see what you come up with. You may break new ground in the field of economics. [Laughter.]

MR. O'LEARY: In view of what the schools of finance have taught, my best advice to the students there is to watch out for the shell.

ISABELLE WEBER, League of Women Voters, Education Fund: Does the panel think the American people believe today there is a serious energy problem facing our country?

CONGRESSMAN UDALL: No, and that is a part of the problem. The question was asked earlier about education and propaganda. There was a Gallup poll that showed a big chunk of the American people do not even know we import oil, and almost half of them do not believe there is a shortage. They think the oil companies are ripping them off, and wells are being capped. We will never get the kind of sacrifice and changing life styles and changing transportation we need to resolve this until the American people feel that there is a crisis.

It is also part of the problem in Congress. We will not vote a standby gas tax because the people back home do not think it is necessary. And people do not believe this, but Congress is not always that far ahead of the American people. We tend to respond to what people are willing to do.

MR. O'LEARY: There is a growing realization around the country, as reflected, for example, in the hearings that preceded the development of the President's energy program, that there is a problem and that sacrifices have to be made to solve it.

MR. LAIRD: I think the American people are far ahead of Congress in this area, and they are ready for strong action in the field of conservation. They are willing to go along with the conservation program. The people in this country look at our balance of payments, and they really understand. The United States will have a $20 billion trade deficit this year. That trade deficit is largely due to oil, some coffee, and a few other little things. But it is largely oil, and the American worker in the factory, the housewife in the home, and the farmer in the field understand that. I think they understand it better than some of our members of Congress do.

BRUCE FEINGERTS, legislative assistant to Senator Russell Long (Democrat, Louisiana): Mr. O'Leary, after you testified before the Senate Finance Committee last week, there was testimony about massive amounts of dissolved natural gas in the waters in the geopressurized zones in Louisiana, in Texas, on the outer continental shelf. Would you approve of a deregulation of the price of this resource in order to encourage its production?

MR. O'LEARY: We have to look at deregulation in these terms: First of all, there is the potential, at least, for substantial increases in production of natural gas from the geopressurized resources in the Gulf of Mexico. Second, we do not know what technology is required to bring it out. The first well, just completed by the Energy Research and Development Administration, indicates that five tons of highly mineralized water—that is, with a lot of salt and other minerals—have to be moved for every thousand cubic feet of gas we get. That is a problem. We cannot let those salts and minerals go into the Gulf because the process could change the whole system in the Gulf.

What has to be done in this case is to consider a substantial incentive price. Whether it will be necessary to go to deregulation, I cannot say at this point. If it takes a price of $4.00 per thousand cubic feet to get a 100-well campaign, I would be prepared to recommend to the President to do it.

MR. LAIRD: The answer, then, is that you would be against deregulation. You would want a fixed price of $4.00?

MR. O'LEARY: Mr. Laird, the reason I have great hesitancy in deregulating a part of the gas market is that all of the plans that have been proposed would maintain controls on a very substantial part of it.

For example, today, the average price of gas in interstate commerce is 65 cents, and that gas is probably worth $2.25. Now, assuming that 90 percent of a gas company's supply costs 65 cents and that it cannot sell its total supply for more than $2.25, what can it afford to pay for the remaining 10 percent of its supply? The answer is well above $10.00 per thousand cubic feet.

That is an aberrant response. In this case, I would much rather negotiate a price with the companies—$3.00, $4.00, or whatever it takes to get this large-scale experiment going. Then we would have a basis for determining the price, rather than relying on the aberrations of a market force in a poison market. The market is poison because 90 percent of that gas company's basic supply would be under controls. That would permit the bidding of a very high price for the small portion they could buy without controls.

JAMES CAREY, Copley News Service: Why is it that three and a half years after the oil embargo of 1973 we still have not had an intelligent debate in this country about what could or could not be accomplished by gasoline rationing? It seems to me that the American people are entitled to know more about this subject, and yet, every time it comes up, people in Congress throw up their hands. They are frightened to death of the subject. We only hear a lot of ideological gobbledygook about how much bureaucracy is involved. I, for one, would like to know what could be accomplished by gasoline rationing.

Mr. Laird: First, I believe in gasoline rationing. I believed it was necessary in order to conserve the product. In a free market, rationing gasoline will have some effect upon price, but that is not the primary factor. As I see what Congress and the administration are doing, they are not encouraging new production of gas and oil, but they are encouraging increased dependence upon petroleum products, particularly gasoline.

If we are to reduce our dependence upon Arab oil, one way is to move rapidly in the direction of gasoline rationing. Certain proposals have been made to this effect. One was rejected almost outright by Congress, but this is one way of making people aware of the problem and of bringing about the conservation that is necessary.

Congressman Udall: We have to do one fundamental thing very soon, and that is to reduce dramatically, or level off at least, the amount of gasoline used by private automobiles. That can be done in several ways. Detroit can be told, as it was a couple of years ago, to produce a fleet of cars that achieve a certain number of miles per gallon by a certain date. That has some advantages—it is fairly simple to administer—and it has some disadvantages.

Another way is through a gasoline tax which forces people to buy small cars and to drive less. People are encouraged to buy smaller cars that go the same number of miles for less gas. At the same time, they are encouraged to drive less, to join carpools, to double up on trips to the store, and so on.

And then there is gas rationing. Now, Mel Laird is right: logically, gas rationing, treating everybody equally, is the fairest way. But rationing is hard to sustain over a long haul. There will be rationing boards, and exemptions for doctors and for people who live involuntarily fifty miles from where they work, and everybody will have a reason for expecting to be excluded. Those who operate resort areas—skiing operations, or summer camps, or summer recreation centers—will say no one will come there under rationing, and that their customers should be exempt. Each little group will have some reason why it should be exempt.

But the fundamental problem with Congress is that no member wants to go home and say, "Re-elect me, dear friends, I'm the guy who gave you gas rationing," when a great majority of constituents do not want gas rationing. So, we have a chicken and an egg. Congressmen ought to lead—we ought to be a little out in front. But if we are out too far in front, we may find ourselves ex-congressmen, and very few of my colleagues want to have that title. [Laughter.]

MR. LAIRD: A gas rationing program should provide a negotiable certificate which can be sold. Then, those who want to go skiing can buy the certificates at a higher price. There are ways of working out problems to avoid a black market and to bring about the necessary conservation. I know it will be tough, but when the oil embargo came about, we were using about 27 percent imported oil, and now we are up to 42 percent. When our balance of trade has a deficit of $20 billion, I begin to believe that drastic conservation measures are necessary.

If we are unwilling to face up to the important decision to create new production—and it looks as though Congress and the administration will not put the emphasis on new wells, on new oil, on new gas, and on the conversion to coal and to nuclear power—then we have to do other things. One of them happens to be gas rationing.

Fred Anderson, executive director, Environmental Law Institute: I encourage free competition among the panelists in answering my question, though I would like particularly to hear from Congressman Udall and Mr. O'Leary.

My question concerns coal. How can it be burned cleanly? How can it be cleaned up to protect the public health, both for miners of coal and for the public at large, after it is burned?

Congressman Udall: There are trade-offs. Everywhere you go you pay a price. Some people say we should go to nuclear power. Nuclear power is clean energy, and nuclear stacks lack the kind of fumes emitted from a coal-fired plant. But nuclear power runs some risks that a lot of people are not willing to run.

If we decide to go slow on nuclear power and burn more coal, it will be necessary to double the production of coal. Some more people will be killed in mines, some will suffer from black lung, and a lot will die of emphysema in Baltimore, Boston, and other places.

Before we plunge into the breeder reactor or some other nuclear technology, we ought to spend money on finding clean ways to burn coal. If we really worked at it, I think we could find how to burn coal cleanly. Like it or not, we will be using a lot more coal in these years ahead.

John Nassikas, lawyer, Cox, Langford, and Brown, and former chairman of the Federal Power Commission: There are many, many commendable aspects of the administration's energy plan, including its conservation aspects and attempts to use economics as a basis for determining the price of depletable resources. One of the problems I have found in the plan, however, is that it falls short of setting the price at the replacement cost at the margin both for natural gas and for the controlled price of oil, though for new crude it is set at the margin.

I also question whether we are accurately stating the replacement cost at the margin if we tie it solely to the world price of crude oil on a B.t.u. equivalent basis. There are other resources that may be substituted for crude oil, at either lesser or greater costs, which affect and are affected by the crude oil price in the world market.

I would like to have your observations, Mr. O'Leary, on how to meet this problem of real economics and real replacement costs under your controlled plan.

MR. DALY: Mr. O'Leary, would you speak in lay terms so that our general audience will be clear on it, too?

MR. O'LEARY: As chairman, until very recently, of the Federal Power Commission, Mr. Nassikas has wrestled with this problem for the last seven or eight years, and it is a fair question.

We appear to be into diminishing returns on conventional oil and gas production in this country. That is to say, we could certainly get more gas production at $4.00 to $5.00 than we will get at $2.00, but unfortunately, as in the case of that Texas example that I gave, not very much more. As we look at the future in regard to energy, we should provide a strong price for oil and gas, and we should get as much as we can reasonably reach. Some calculations indicate that we can get a fair return by raising the price of natural gas to $1.75 per thousand cubic feet and the price of oil to $13.50 per barrel. But we would not get much more if we were to raise the price another dollar for gas and another $5.00 for oil. So figuring a price is the first thing we have to do.

The second is to begin to look at high cost alternatives. I am a strong advocate of moving fast on coal gasification. Gas obtained that way will cost $4.00 per thousand cubic feet, but we should not advance the whole market to $4.00. That would reward people who are doing very little for us—no more than shallow drilling for relatively cheap sources of gas.

We should look at this problem in nonmarket terms. We have to get as much gas as we reasonably can. Then we have to get as much of the liquified natural gas as we reasonably can. Then we have to get coal gas at the lowest reasonable price. If instead of doing that we accept the classicial economists' view of market clearing, I am afraid we would soon be paying $5.00 per thousand cubic feet, rather than the $1.75 proposed under the President's plan, and we would not get much more gas.

PROFESSOR MITCHELL: As I listened to Mr. O'Leary speak, I believe I understood why we have an energy crisis. The costs of producing these various energy resources cannot be known in advance. The Federal Power Commission, particularly under Chairman Nassikas's predecessors, attempted to do this. Economists generally regard that to have been a rather ludicrous affair.

On the basis not only of economic theory but also of the whole history of the Federal Power Commission, I find it difficult to believe that anyone could seriously propose we can do that kind of thing—that anyone can pick out different sources of natural gas, predict in advance what the costs will be, and set prices for gas in different places or at different depths.

DEMING COWLES, legislative assistant to Senator Mike Gravel (Democrat, Alaska): My question centers on last week's hearings by the Senate Finance Committee, which were referred to earlier. There have been reports by the National Petroleum Council that there are significant quantities of oil and gas available in this country, and there have been similar studies by the Energy Research and Development Administration. On the other hand, Mr. O'Leary mentioned tonight that the technological improvement of solar energy has been so great and so rapid that we may have economical solar energy soon. In light of the costs, both environmental and capital, of conversion to coal, why adopt a program, such as the President has proposed, of converting dramatically to coal, and then shifting to nuclear power, when alternative sources such as solar energy appear to be available soon? There are sufficient reserves of oil and gas for the near term.

MR. O'LEARY: A very good question. I think the answer is relatively straightforward. Today we do what economics and technology permit. That is to say, we do not have solar energy quite yet. We may have it in five years, more probably in fifteen, as an economic proposition. We cannot wait until that time to make the investment in, for example, solar generation. We will need the power three years from now, or four years from now, or ten years from now. That means we have to proceed with what we have.

However, we should always keep our eye on that next technological leap and push toward it as hard as we can, using the free enterprise system. Incidentally, the cost of solar energy has been reduced so dramatically not by government laboratories but by people out looking for a buck. The government is a part of this process, to be sure, targeting on the right things to do and doing them as sensibly as possible.

But the bottom line on your question is, unfortunately, for the next ten years we have no alternative to nuclear energy and coal. We will have increased power requirements under almost any set of assumptions that may be proposed, even though we are doing our best to conserve. Consequently, we will have to work with the technology at hand.

RONALD SHEINMAN, System Automation Corporation: Gentlemen, what impact will the President's energy program have on the overall U.S. economy in terms of gross national product, employment, inflation, and the like? Can any of you give us some figures?

PROFESSOR MITCHELL: I cannot give any figures. I do not know if anybody else can.

MR. O'LEARY: I can give you the figures that have been developed by the application of the Project Independence Evaluation System model to the problem, although it is fair to say that it is difficult to project, even in a macro sense, the impact of a program of this scope. The inflationary effect will be negligible, less than 0.5 percent. There will be a nondiscernible impact upon employment. We simply cannot find it. And the GNP will be about 0.3 percent below what it might otherwise be. All in all, we find significant adjustments within the system but no major changes in the large measures of how the economy is doing.

MR. LAIRD: I think it is very difficult to give projections like that.

MR. O'LEARY: I agree.

MR. LAIRD: I do not believe that anyone can. As far as OPEC is concerned, this program gives them complete freedom to raise their prices. There will be no real competition from U.S. production in oil and gas.

Talk about converting to solar power which may occur perhaps in ten years, discourages the tough decision making that is needed right now in the United States. It is unrealistic to talk about solar power for ten years. But no one can predict the impact on gross national product or on inflation at this time.

CARROL GADDY, Tenneco: Congressman Udall, a couple of times this evening you have mentioned the possibility of breaking up the oil companies. How do you think breaking up the oil companies would affect the energy problem? And who is going to bear the costs of breaking up the oil companies? Is it not true that they would probably be passed on to the consumer?

CONGRESSMAN UDALL: Yes, what we will pass on to the consumer will be lower prices, or at least prices which do not increase as rapidly as they have in the past. We have been told that we will not have the energy we need unless we let it be produced by the giant oil companies. They are not satisfied with just running out of oil. They are buying up most of the coal and uranium, and they are getting into geothermal energy. They are into every conceivable kind of energy production.

I would divest them through an act of Congress if I had the power, but divestiture has been given a bad name by Bob Hope and Mobil and everybody else. I am not sure we have the horses to do that just yet. But I have proposed a first step in the Congress, that is, that the federal energy reserves—the offshore oil and gas, the western coal, the geothermal resources, the uranium on federal lands—belong to the people and will be leased to those who will compete, to those who know what a free market really is.

The coal will be leased to independent coal companies. The federal oil will be leased to the independent oil companies, and we will let them make some money producing it. That would provide competition and lower prices.

In 1911, the government broke up Standard Oil, the old Rockefeller trust that had most of the oil in America. Standard Oil was broken up into thirty-three companies. And the sun came up, babies were born, weddings were held, and they celebrated Mother's Day and the World Series. The world did not come to an end.

In fact, two years later, the stockholders did not have $600 in one share, they had $900 in thirty-three shares. The break-up was good for consumers, good for the public, good for stockholders. It was even good for oil executives, because instead of being third vice presidents in a big octopus, they were heading up their own little companies and competing—not just talking competition, but practicing it and trying new and innovative things. The best thing that could happen to this country would be to break up the oil companies and to get back to true competition.

PROFESSOR MITCHELL: Congressman Udall is rewriting history with regard to the Standard Oil trust. In virtually every case, the companies that were broken up reintegrated vertically. Further, I have never seen any evidence that prices suddenly plummeted as a consequence of the new development of competition in the industry.

I have made a study myself of what would happen if we broke up the major vertically integrated oil companies. The conclusion, which seems to me to be inevitable, is that the profits of those companies will have to rise, because in every case the companies will become riskier ventures. They will therefore have to pay more for the money they borrow, and they will have to earn higher rates of return on equity. Ironically, what would happen if the oil companies were broken up, either horizontally or vertically, is that big oil profits would get bigger, in my estimation by about 20 percent. I do not see any other possibility.

CONGRESSMAN UDALL: What oil companies have told us is, yes, they are great big companies, and yes, they do dominate oil, and yes, they do run all the way from the wellhead to the gas station, but the American people cannot do a thing about it. They are just too big. We will not get the new energy we need unless we let them produce it. We cannot stop them from going into coal. We cannot stop them from going into uranium and all the other competing sources.

In this free market we have heard so much about tonight, a refinery that has a product to sell would have salesmen out everywhere, sharpening their pencils, and trying to get the most for their product. And all kinds of people out

42

there would be sharpening their pencils, trying to get the gasoline cheaper, either from me or from another refinery.

That situation does not exist today. Instead, we have the big oil companies: they run their own refineries and have their own marketing facilities. There is no attempt and no obligation to compete. Competition is what divestiture is all about. The people who preach competition the most would not recognize it if they saw it on Wall Street at high noon. [Laughter.]

PROFESSOR MITCHELL: Are you aware, Congressman Udall, that West Germany and Japan, among others, are merging companies in an attempt to put together organizations like the vertically integrated oil companies in the United States because these companies are recognized as being so efficient? There are economies of vertical integration. It is true, I have to confess, that my profession has not seriously researched those economies until very recently. But economists have done so recently, and the results show that economies of operation in vertically integrated companies exist, as it happens, in the oil industry.

I have no particular reason to want oil companies to be big or to be vertically integrated, but it is an economical way of doing business in that industry. It will always be an economical way.

MR. LAIRD: The problem that bothers me about Congressman Udall's little fairy tale is that it does not address the problem we are discussing today. We are trying to move towards a solution to the energy problem, and his suggestion has nothing to do with solving the energy problem.

CONGRESSMAN UDALL: It is the very core of it. The energy problem will not be solved unless there is competition, so that every kind of device and idea—solar, uranium, biomass, wind power, everything—can compete. And they cannot compete when a few big oil companies dominate all the competing kinds of energy.

Mr. Laird: They cannot compete as long as the government sets the prices.

Congressman Udall: Either we will have regulation, or we will have competition. When the companies are very big, they are asking for regulation. I want to make them little and have competition.

Don Sider, *Time* magazine: It has been suggested that between the call to the moral equivalent of war on a Monday night last April and the Friday press conference in which the President told us we would all get a fat rebate if we did not drive too much, something was lost. Can the panel tell us what they think the American people will go for? How far will the American people go in regimentation or mandated savings of energy?

Mr. O'Leary: I think that the American people will go further than the Congress will permit them to at this time. We have to recognize that this is really the first round in what will be the main event in the next Congress and the next Congress and the next Congress.

I agree, incidentally, with Mr. Laird that the American people are ahead of Congress and may be ahead of us in the executive branch. I do not think that we will get as tough a program as we proposed, and I do not think that the American people would cavil at accepting a tougher program than the one we proposed. So we will lose two ways here.

Over the next three or four years, as the American people begin to get a better idea of where we are in the world—with the $20 billion deficit we are running this year, the enormously increased dependence upon imports and upon OPEC within the import total, and the threat represented by that to the whole way of life of this economy—they will accept whatever needs to be done to keep us whole.

44

Mr. Daly: This concludes another public policy forum presented by the American Enterprise Institute for Public Policy Research. On behalf of AEI, our heartfelt thanks to the distinguished panelists: Professor Mitchell, the Honorable Melvin R. Laird, Congressman Morris K. Udall, and Federal Energy Administrator John O'Leary, and also, our thanks to our guests and experts in the audience for their participation.

Cover and design: Pat Taylor